Introducción

Jack, Tom y Danny son tres amigos a los que su profesora les ha encargado que escriban una historia de miedo, pero a ellos no se les ocurre nada. Entonces deciden ir al cementerio el sábado por la noche para buscar fantasmas. Cuando llegan allí se encuentran con que es un lugar oscuro y silencioso. Pero eso no es todo, empiezan a ocurrir cosas raras y los chicos se topan con unos fantasmas muy peculiares. ¡Esta espeluznante aventura les proporciona una gran cantidad de material sobre el que escribir!

Introducció

En Jack, en Tom i en Danny són tres amics als quals la seva mestra els ha encarregat escriure una història de por, però no se'ls acut res. Llavors, decideixen anar al cementiri dissabte al vespre per buscar fantasmes. Quan hi arriben troben que és un indret fosc i silenciós. Però això no és tot, comencen a passar coses estranyes i els nois ensopeguen amb uns fantasmes molt peculiars. Aquesta esgarrifosa aventura els proporcionarà molt material per escriure!

Sarrera

Jack, Tom eta Danny hiru adiskide dira, eta irakasleak beldurrezko istorio bat idazteko eskatu die, baina ez zaie ezer bururatzen. Orduan, larunbat gauean hilerrira joatea erabaki dute, mamuak bilatzeko. Hara iristen direnean, ordea, leku ilun eta isil bat aurkitzen dute. Baina hori ez da dena; gauza arraroak gertatzen hasten dira, eta mutilek oso mamu xelebreekin egiten dute topo. Abentura ile-lazgarri honetatik eskuratzen duten material pilarekin, badute zertaz idatzi!

Limiar

Jack, Tom e Danny son tres amigos ós que a súa profesora lles encargou que escriban unha historia de medo, pero a eles non se lles ocorre nada. Daquela deciden ir ó cemiterio o sábado pola noite á procura de pantasmas. Ó chegaren alí encóntranse con que é un lugar escuro e silandeiro. Mais iso non é todo, comezan a ocorrer cousas raras e os rapaces atópanse cunhas pantasmas moi peculiares. ¡Esta arrepiante aventura fornécelles unha gran cantidade de material sobre o que escribir!

The Mystery of the Tomb

Chapter 1: Friday Afternoon

It was four o'clock on Friday afternoon. The bell rang and the students in class 5 started running out of the classroom. Their teacher, Miss Wilson, was at her table.

Jack ran quickly out of the classroom with his friends, Danny and Tom. The boys liked Miss Wilson, but they were very happy that it was Friday afternoon and that it was time to go home. Friday was always the best day of the school week.

What must the students do for Miss Wilson?

A

B

C

Chapter 2: A Problem

"What are you going to write about in your story?" Jack asked Tom.

"I don't know," said Tom. "It's difficult for me to think of a scary story. ***I'm not frightened of*** anything! What can I write about?"

Jack thought for a moment. "I don't know what we can write about," he said. "What are we going to do?"

"I've got an idea!" said Tom. "Let's do something scary this weekend! We can do something on Saturday night! Then we can write our stories on Sunday."

"Yes, that's a good idea!" said Danny. "But what can we do?"

Tom and Jack thought for a moment.

Suddenly, Jack had an idea.

"OK. Let's ***meet outside*** the cemetery before midnight tomorrow and we'll try to find something scary – maybe a ***ghost***!" said Jack.

The boys smiled. They were very happy with their plan, and there was nothing to be frightened of. After all, ghosts don't exist, do they?

What do the boys decide to do on Saturday night?

Chapter 3: In the Street

The next night, at 11.45, Jack, Tom and Danny were in the street outside the cemetery. It was very ***dark*** and there weren't any lights in the houses. The boys looked through the ***gates*** of the cemetery.

Jack didn't have a plan. "I don't know," he said. "Let's wait ten minutes. Maybe I'll think of something. Then we'll go into the cemetery."

The moon appeared from behind a cloud and the boys saw strange figures near the gates. Jack tried to be ***brave***. "There's nothing to be frightened of," he thought. "It's only a cemetery, with lots of trees, ***grass***, long ***paths*** and ***graves***…"

"Aaargghh!" shouted Tom, suddenly.

Jack and Danny jumped. "Tom! Are you OK?" asked Danny.

"Something ***bit*** my leg," Tom answered. He examined his leg. "It's nothing. I'm OK," he said.

"Phew!" said Jack. "You frightened me! Don't do that again!"

"Are you frightened, Tom?" asked Danny.

"No, I'm not," answered Tom. "Why?"

"Because I can see something in the trees!" said Danny.

The boys looked at the tree and saw … a small black cat. The cat jumped from the tree and ***ran past*** them.

Where did the boys see the cat?

"We're being stupid," said Jack. "There's nothing to be frightened of, OK?"

"OK," said Tom and Danny.

"I know," said Jack. "She baked the best biscuits in the world. She was a fantastic grandmother."

He was sad for a moment, then he asked, "Did anybody bring a ***torch***?"

"No," said Tom and Danny.

"Hmmmm, I forgot to bring a torch, too," said Jack. "But it's not important. Let's make a plan."

"How many paths are there in the cemetery?" asked Tom.

"Three," answered Jack. "One path goes round the cemetery and two paths go through it. We can each take a different path. Then we can meet at the big, black tomb in the middle. It's bigger than the other tombs. You'll recognise it easily."

Tom and Danny were worried. Five minutes was a long time in a dark cemetery.

"And remember," said Jack, "we must all be at the big, black tomb in the middle at midnight!"

The boys ***climbed over*** the gates: first Jack, then Tom, then Danny.

Where are the boys going to meet?

A

B

C

Chapter 4: In the Cemetery

It was very dark and silent inside the cemetery. Jack looked at his watch.

Tom took the path on the left. "See you later!" he said and walked quietly along the path.

Danny ***pointed to*** the path on the right. "I'll go that way, round the cemetery, Jack," he said. "But I'm frightened. Maybe I'll see a ghost. What will I do?"

"***Shout loudly*** and run very quickly!" said Jack with a smile.

"Good luck!" said Danny. "See you soon!"

"I must take the middle path," thought Jack. "I don't like this!"

Jack tried to see into the ***darkness***. Then he started to walk along the middle path.

Which path does each boy take?

Suddenly, a cloud passed in front of the moon. Jack stopped and waited. "It's so dark without the moon!" he thought. He started to hear noises ***all round him***.

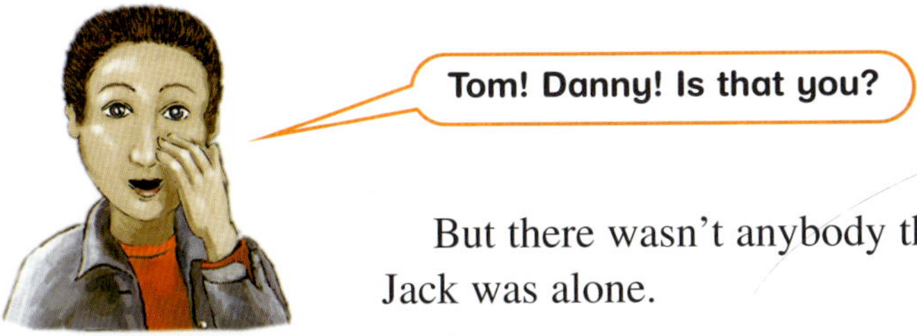

But there wasn't anybody there. Jack was alone.

Then he remembered a scary film about a cemetery he once saw on television. He remembered the scary book he read the week before, too.

Suddenly, something touched his head and he jumped, but it was only the branch of a tree.

The moon appeared again. "I can see now!" thought Jack. But when he got near the big, black tomb, he started to imagine things again.

Jack walked slowly. He was very frightened. The tomb was directly in front of him now. It was big and black and scary and it was very quiet. Jack walked slowly to the tomb.

Then suddenly, he heard a noise. The noise came from the tomb!

What does Jack imagine? Choose the correct pictures.

Chapter 5: The Ghost

Jack was terrified. Suddenly, he heard a noise and the door of the tomb started to open slowly. A white figure appeared at the door.

Suddenly, Jack heard the church clock.

Jack ran very quickly to a big tree. He jumped behind the tree and tried to ***hide***, but he ***bumped into something*** behind the tree. The thing moved!

"Aaargghh!" Jack shouted. "What … what are you?" The thing put a hand over Jack's mouth.

Jack tried to escape.

Jack looked and saw that the 'thing' was Tom and Danny.

"Yes!" said Tom and Danny. They were very frightened.

The three boys watched the white figure come slowly out of the tomb and move towards them. They heard strange, loud noises. CLANK! CLANK!

"It's a ghost!" said Tom. "And it's got lots of ***chains***!"

The noises got louder. CLANK! CLANK!

What does Jack want to do?

The boys climbed the tree. A cloud covered the moon again for a short time and the night was very dark.

Suddenly, the ghost bumped into a small tomb and fell on the grass.

The three boys looked ***at each other***. "Did you hear that?" said Danny quietly.

The ghost tried to stand up. "Ow! My leg!" it said again.

The three boys climbed down from the tree and stood behind it. They looked at the 'ghost' and saw that a white ***sheet*** covered it. Suddenly, a ***shiny gold ring*** appeared from under the white sheet and ***rolled along*** the grass.

"Stupid ring!" said a man's voice. The 'ghost' ***took off*** the white sheet and stood up.

"Wow!" said Tom. "It isn't a ghost! It's a short, fat man!"

The man wore black trousers and a black sweater and he had a big, black bag in his hand. He took the shiny gold ring from the grass and he put it in the black bag. The bag was full of shiny things and the boys saw that it was very heavy.

What can the boys see in the bag? Choose the correct pictures.

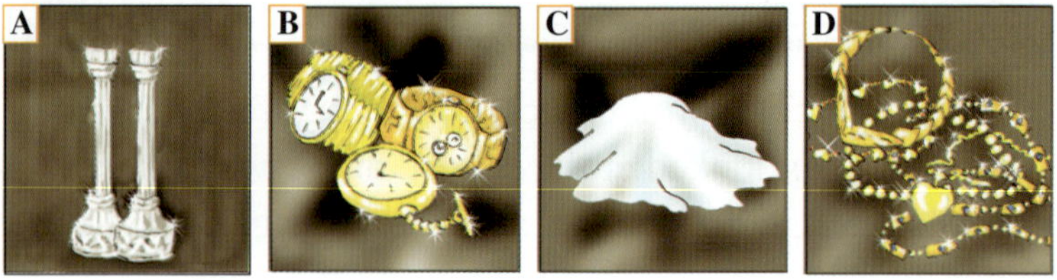

Chapter 6: An Idea

The boys heard another man's voice near one of the tombs. "Is that you, Bill?" said the voice. "Quick! We haven't got all night!"

Bill, the burglar, walked towards the tomb.

The boys saw the other man, Joe, standing near the tomb. Joe was tall and thin and he wore black trousers and a black sweater, too.

Then the two men started to run to the gates.

Then Jack saw the white sheet on the grass. "Hmmm," he said. "I've got an idea."

The two burglars, Bill and Joe, often worked together.

The week before, at night, they went into the houses near the cemetery and they stole lots of things.

Then they hid everything in one of the tombs.

Now the two men were at the gates. Joe climbed over the gates. Bill started to follow him but suddenly, he heard a noise, "Whhhoooooohhh!"

Where was Bill when he heard the noise?

A

B

C

Chapter 7: Jack and Tom Try to Escape

"Aaarrrrgghh!" said Bill. A tall white figure stood in front of him. It made a loud noise again, "Whhoooohhh!"

Bill fell on the grass and looked up at the 'ghost'.

Bill was very frightened. He didn't believe in ghosts, but the white figure was very tall and scary.

"OK! Take the bag!" said Bill. "Take it! I don't want it!"

"Bill! What are you doing?" shouted Joe from outside the gates. "Don't be stupid! That isn't a ghost! It's two boys and they're wearing your white sheet!"

Bill stood up and looked at the 'ghost'. He walked all round the tall white figure. The 'ghost' didn't move. Then Bill saw a pair of legs under the sheet.

He ***pulled the bottom*** of the sheet very hard.

The sheet fell on the grass and Jack and Tom fell on the grass, too.

Bill was very angry.

Jack and Tom stood up quickly and tried to escape from Bill. They ran round trees and climbed over tombs, but Bill followed them. He was fat but he ran very quickly.

Bill was very near Jack and Tom. Suddenly, Jack fell over a stone on the path.

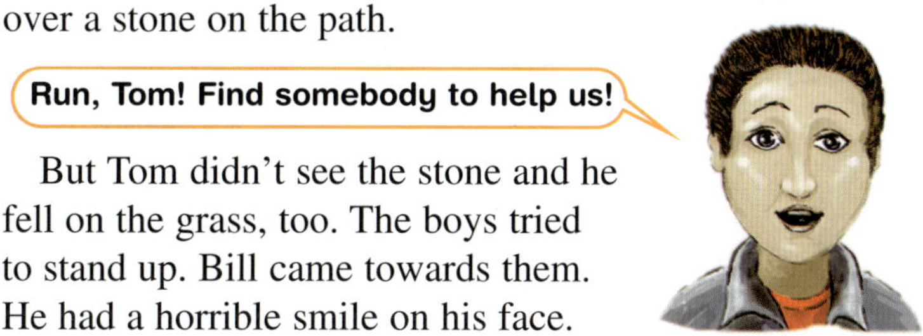

But Tom didn't see the stone and he fell on the grass, too. The boys tried to stand up. Bill came towards them. He had a horrible smile on his face.

"You can't escape now," he said. "I'll teach you a lesson! You won't go to a cemetery in the middle of the night again!"

Why did Tom fall?

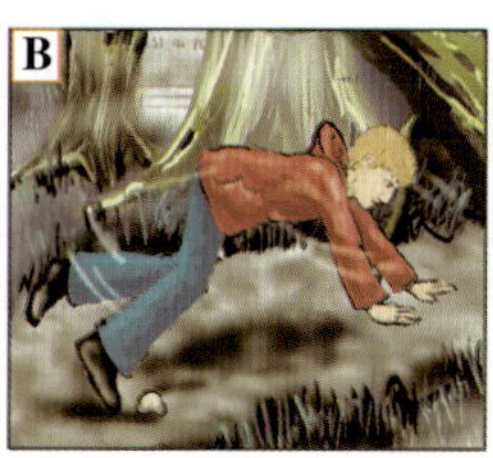

Chapter 8: Strange Events

Suddenly, there was a bright light all round them and an old woman appeared in front of the boys. She was small and thin, she had white hair and she wore a red ***dressing gown***. There was a bright light all round her head and she was very angry. Jack and Tom were very surprised.

Bill put his hands in front of his eyes. "Who are you?" he asked.

Jack looked carefully at the old woman.

Grandma Mackay opened her mouth. "DON'T TOUCH MY GRANDSON!" she said to Bill in a terrible, loud voice.

"Aaaarrrgggh! It's a ghost!" said Bill and he tried to escape. But Grandma Mackay raised her arms above her head. All the trees in the cemetery started to move from side to side and there was a loud, strong wind. Suddenly, the wind caught Bill and took him towards the cemetery gates.

Grandma Mackay pointed her long, thin finger at the top of the cemetery gates. Surprised, Jack and Tom watched the wind take Bill to the top of the gates. Bill's black sweater ***stuck*** to the top of the gates and he ***hung*** there, very frightened.

Jack and Tom started to laugh.

"Grandma, you're fantastic!" shouted Jack.

What happened to Bill?

Jack looked out of the cemetery gates. He saw Joe running down the road. "Quick, Grandma!" said Jack. "You must do something! The other man is escaping!"

"Oh no, he isn't!" said Grandma Mackay and she smiled at Jack. Then she pointed her finger again. The wind followed Joe down the road, caught him and took him back to the cemetery gates.

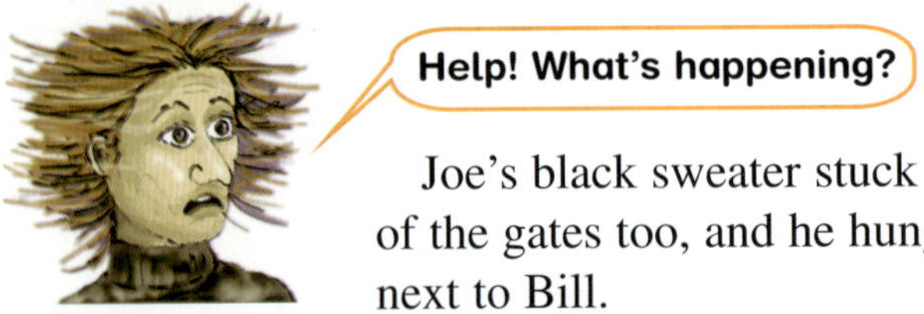

Joe's black sweater stuck to the top of the gates too, and he hung there, next to Bill.

Suddenly, the wind disappeared. "I hope that was a lesson for them!" said Grandma Mackay.

At that moment, Danny appeared from behind a tree and ran towards the boys.

Then Danny saw the ghostly figure of Grandma Mackay, and he stopped. "Wow!" he said. "You're Jack's grandmother! You always baked delicious biscuits for us when we visited you."

Grandma Mackay smiled at the boys affectionately.

"Can you stay and talk to us for an hour or two, Grandma?" asked Jack.

"No, I can't. I must go now," answered Grandma Mackay. "The police are coming. I don't want to be here when they arrive. Goodbye, Jack."

Grandma Mackay disappeared.

Chapter 9: The Police Arrive

The boys watched two police cars arrive at the cemetery. The cars made a lot of noise and the noise woke up most of the people in the houses.

The people saw Bill and Joe on the cemetery gates and the big black bag on the grass next to them.

One of the people saw a gold necklace at the top of the black bag.

Everybody was very angry. Four policemen got out of the police cars and walked to the gates.

Why is everybody angry?

The policemen looked at the two men on the gates.

A policeman saw the white sheet. He took it and showed it to the other policemen.

Everybody started to laugh.

Two policemen took Bill and Joe from the gates, put them into one of the police cars and left.

The other two policemen stayed with the boys. The boys were ***tired*** now after their adventure in the cemetery.

"Can we go home now?" asked Jack.

"Yes," said one of the policemen. "We'll take you home. And there will be a ***reward*** for you, too. You caught the two burglars! Bill Watson and Joe Prescott burgled lots of houses. You'll be heroes at school on Monday! You're all very brave. Now let's phone your parents and tell them what happened."

The boys smiled.

What's going to happen to the boys? Choose the correct pictures.

A

B

C

D

Chapter 10: At Home

On the way home, Jack was very sad. He missed Grandma Mackay very much. "I wanted to talk to her in the cemetery," he thought. "I wanted to tell her things, but she disappeared." He looked out of the car window for a moment.

"Goodbye," said Danny. "See you tomorrow." He got out of the police car and went into his house.

"Yes, see you tomorrow," said Jack and Tom.

When Jack got home, he told his parents about the burglars, but he didn't tell them about Grandma Mackay.

Jack went upstairs to his bedroom and got into bed. "I can smell perfume, the perfume of roses," he thought. He remembered that Grandma Mackay always used rose perfume.

Jack was tired, but it was impossible to sleep. He looked out of the window at the stars.

Jack can't sleep. What does he do?

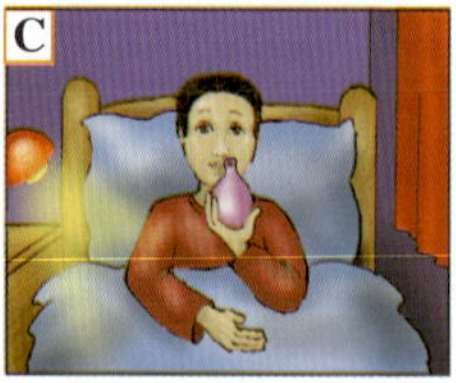

Jack sat up, ***put on*** the light and read a book for a few minutes. When he ***lay down*** again, he felt something under his pillow. He looked under the pillow and he saw a silver box.

"Where did that come from?" he thought.

Jack opened the box carefully. "Wow!" he said, surprised.

The box was full of Jack's favourite biscuits.

Jack smiled, took one of the biscuits and ate it.

Then he lay down in bed and fell asleep.

English	Castellano	Català
meet outside	quedar fuera de	trobar-se fora de
necklaces	collares	collarets
paths	caminos	camins
pillows	almohadas	coixins
pointed to	señaló hacia	va assenyalar
pulled the bottom	tiró de la parte de abajo	va tirar de la part de sota
put on	encendió	va encendre
ran past	pasó corriendo por delante de	va passar corrent davant de
reward	recompensa	recompensa
rolled along	rodó por	va rodolar per
scary	de miedo	de por
sheet	sábana	llençol
shiny gold ring	reluciente anillo de oro	lluent anell d'or
shout loudly	grita fuerte	crida fort
silver candlesticks	candelabros de plata	canelobres de plata
stuck	se enganchó	es va enganxar
tired	cansados	cansats
took off	se quitó	va treure's
torch	linterna	lot
towards	hacia	cap a
tried to make a fool of me	trataban de reírse de mí	intentaven burlar-se de mi
witch	bruja	bruixa

English	Euskara	Galego
meet outside	-ren kanpoaldean elkartzekotan gelditu	quedar fóra de
necklaces	lepokoak	colares
paths	bide-zidorrak	camiños
pillows	burkoak	almofadas
pointed to	-rantz seinalatu zuen	sinalou cara a
pulled the bottom	azpitik tiratu zion	tirou da parte de abaixo
put on	piztu zuen	acendeu
ran past	aurretik lasterka igaro zitzaien	pasou correndo por diante de
reward	ordainsaria	recompensa
rolled along	-an biraka erori zen	rolou por
scary	beldurrezko	de medo
sheet	maindirea	saba
shiny gold ring	urrezko eraztun distiratsua	relucente anel de ouro
shout loudly	oihukatu ozenki	berra forte
silver candlesticks	zilarrezko argimutilak	candelabros de prata
stuck	katigatu zen	enganchouse
tired	nekatuak	cansos
took off	erantzi zuen	quitou
torch	esku-argia	lanterna
towards	aldera, -ganantz	cara a
tried to make a fool of me	ni barregarri utzi nahian zebiltzan	trataban de rir de min
witch	sorgina	bruxa

The Mystery of the Tomb

by Marisa McGreevy

Burlington Books
P. O. Box 54411
3721 Limassol
Cyprus
Burlington Books is an imprint of Danos Books Ltd.

The publisher would like to thank the following people:

Castellano: Mª Paz Yagüe Sarmiento
Català: Maria Esteve Serraviñals
Euskara: Joan Ignazio Bereziartua Iraola
Galego: Ramón Nicolás Rodríguez

ISBN 9963-46-571-4

Burlington Reader No. E2.08

10 9

11 10 09